Learning Resource Services   **The College** of West Anglia

Call 01553 815306 to renew your books or if you have any queries.
You can also renew or reserve books by going to
http://library.cwa.ac.uk/
The card holder is responsible for the safe keeping and return of this item. Fines will be charged on all late items.

WORLD ORGANIZATIONS

The European Union

Jillian Powell

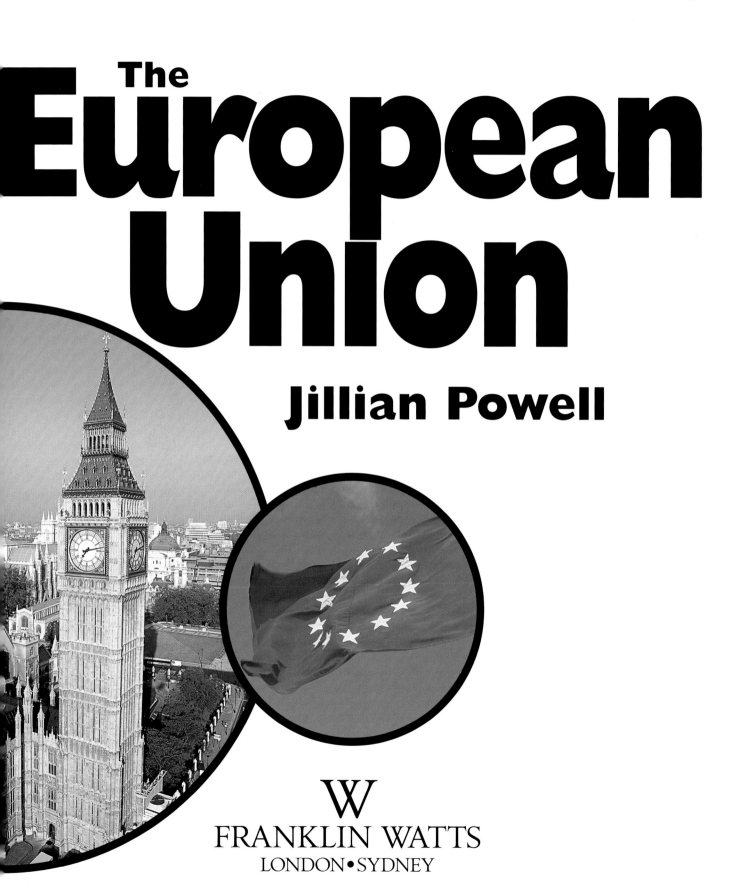

W

FRANKLIN WATTS
LONDON•SYDNEY

First published in 2001
by Franklin Watts, 96 Leonard Street
London EC2A 4XD

Franklin Watts Australia
56 O'Riordan Street
Alexandria NSW 2015

Series editor: Anderley Moore
Designer: Simon Borrough
Picture research: Sue Mennell
Consultant: Graham Welch, European Commission

This title was produced with the European
Commission's advice, but the views expressed within
do not necessarily reflect the views of the European
Commission.

A CIP catalogue record for this book is
available from the British Library.

ISBN   0 7496 3694 7

Dewey classification 341.24
Printed in Malaysia

Picture credits: Cover: Impact, Tony Page
(main), Panos, Chris Sattlberger (top right),
EU (bottom right). Inside: CCE: 20;
Courtesy of Temple Bar Properties: 12
(bottom). Holt Studios: 14 (bottom), 15
(bottom) Nigel Cattlin. Impact: 3 (top and
bottom), 13 W. Louvet, 17 (bottom) Simon
Shepheard, 25. Popperfoto: 2 (top and
centre), 4, 5 (top), 7 Yves Herman, 8 (bottom)
Vincent Kessler, 9 (bottom) Olivier Hoslet, 12
(top), 19 (top) Pascal Rossignol, 19 (bottom)
Ian Hodgson, 22 Benoit Doppagne, 24 (top), 24
(bottom) Kai Pfaffenbach, 26 Achim Bieniek, 29
Vincent Kessler. Rex Features: 6 Martin Lee, 11
Lehtikuva/Markku, 16 (top) J. Sutton, 18 (right), 23
Tim Norman, 27. RSPB Images: 29 Andrew Hay. Still
Pictures: 17 (top) Hartmut Scwarzbach, 18 (left) John
Maier, 28 Jo Elms/Christian Aid. Topham 5 (bottom) AP, 9
(top), 10 Richard Laird, 14 (top), 15 (top), 16 (bottom)
Barry Batchelor.

Contents

1. Why was the European Union formed?

After the Second World War (1939–45) in which 55 million people died, governments began to look for ways of building closer links between the countries of Europe to prevent further wars.

In 1951, six European countries (France, Belgium, West Germany, Luxembourg, Italy and the Netherlands) set up the European Coal and Steel Community (ECSC). Its aim was to protect the interests of their steel and coal industries. In 1957 they joined together to form the European Economic Community (EEC) by signing the Treaty of Rome.

▼ European leaders meet to sign the Treaty of Rome in 1957.

EU member states and year of joining

1957
Belgium
France
West Germany
Italy
Luxembourg
Netherlands

1973
United Kingdom
Ireland
Denmark

1981
Greece

1986
Portugal
Spain

1995
Austria
Finland
Sweden

Growth of the European Union

During the 1970s and 80s, more countries applied to join the European Community. From 1979, direct elections were held for the European Parliament. This meant that Europeans could vote every five years for the Members of European Parliament (MEPs) they wanted to represent them.

In 1992, the 12 member states signed the Treaty on European Union, agreeing to work to develop the Community into a political, economic and monetary union and in doing so, also changing its name.

During its history, the EU has grown in size and power. Enlargement will continue as more countries in central and eastern Europe join.

▼ *Like all citizens of Europe, UK citizens hold a European-format passport.*

▲ *European Union heads of state get together in 1999 to discuss the crisis in Kosovo.*

▲ *The flag of the EU has a circle of stars representing the union of member states.*

Today, the European Union still aims to promote peace in Europe. It is also involved in trying to raise the standard of living for all EU citizens, improving trade and spreading European wealth more evenly. The EU has its own emblem and anthem, and Europe Day is celebrated every year on 9th May in member states.

The countries that have joined the EU are known as 'member states'. They work to improve living and working conditions, to represent Europe to the rest of the world, and to give their peoples the benefit of European rulings on citizens' rights.

All member states have democratic governments – these are governments that are elected by their people. There are now 15 member states of the EU, mostly from western Europe, and other central and eastern European countries have applied to join.

Main aims of the EU

- To form a closer union between European peoples
- To improve their working and living conditions
- To get rid of barriers to trade between member states
- To allow people, goods, services and money to move freely throughout the Union

EU citizens

The European Union has more than doubled since the Treaty of Rome was signed in 1957 – the point that marks the official beginning of the European Union. There are now around 370 million EU citizens. Anyone who is a citizen of a member state is also a citizen of the EU.

 ## Spotlight

Since 1985, each year the Council of Ministers of Culture of the EU has chosen a "cultural capital of Europe". The city is given grants to develop culture and the arts for its people and visitors. There were nine European Cities of Culture in the year 2000: Avignon, Bergen, Bologna, Brussels, Cracow, Helsinki, Prague, Reykjavik and Santiago de Compostella.

▲ *Celebrations in Brussels, one of the nine European cities of culture chosen in 2000.*

 ## Spotlight

A wide range of languages is spoken in the EU. All legislation, formal and other documents are prepared in the 11 official languages of the 15 member states. English and French are most often used for meetings. A team of interpreters translates each language at official meetings. Translated EU documents are colour coded: for example, papers in English are pink, papers in French are blue. In the Court of Justice, a language of the case is chosen and translation and interpretation are provided.

European citizens have the right:

- to move and live anywhere within the EU
- to vote and stand in local government and European Parliament elections
- to be helped if in trouble when travelling in non-EU countries
- to petition and appeal to the European Ombudsman (the highest official)

The European Union is run by representatives from its member states. Member states take it in turn to hold the Presidency of the EU for six months. Portugal held it at from 1 January to 30 June 2000, for example.

The European Commission

One of the EU's institutions, the European Commission, has 20 Commissioners selected from each country in the EU. Its main job is to make sure that the policies written down in the Treaties are carried out and to defend the interests of EU citizens. The Commission is based in Brussels, and its staff work in Brussels and Luxembourg. Its President is nominated by member state governments and approved by the European Parliament. He or she will usually hold office for 5 years. From the middle of the year 2000, Romano Prodi of Italy held the post.

▶ *Romano Prodi, President of the European Commission, at a news conference in Strasbourg.*

The Council of Ministers

The Council, based in Brussels, is the highest decision-making organization within the EU and the most powerful of its institutions. There are 15 ministers in the Council. On particularly important decisions, every member must agree. Any member state, however small, can block a decision in the Council.

The European Parliament

The 370 million European citizens of the EU are represented by the European Parliament. There are 626 members of the European Parliament (MEPs), each directly elected by the people in their European Constituency (the area that they represent) for five-year terms. The number of members from each member state is based on

▲ The European Parliament buildings in Strasbourg.

the size of its population. The Parliament meets in Strasbourg and its staff, the Secretariat, work in Luxembourg. It debates proposals from the Commission and the Council and watches over the work of the Commission.

◄ Members of the European Parliament (MEPs) meet at a session of the European Parliament in Brussels.

The multi-layered system of EU government can be loosely compared with the US Constitution, which has a supreme national government under an elected President, and many state governments and smaller units governing states, cities and towns. This means that the balance of power is evenly distributed and reduces the likelihood of corruption at the top.

Spotlight

If MEPs are concerned about any area of EU policy, they can hold question and answer sessions with members of the Commission. In March 2000, the Agriculture Committee of the European Parliament put questions to the Environment Commissioner Margot Walström. They were concerned that EU policies aimed at reducing the amount of nitrates in the environment were not taking effect. MEPs argued that there had been delays because the EU had not considered the cost to farmers.

The European Ombudsman

An Ombudsman is like a watchdog and he or she can receive complaints from any European citizen against any EU institution. The Ombudsman investigates complaints and suggests changes or improvements in the way things are done. The European Ombudsman is appointed by the Parliament.

◀ *The White House, Washington, home of the President of the United States governement. The government structure of the EU has been likened to that of the United States.*

 Finland's EU flag flying at the Senate Square in Helsinki. Finland held the EU Presidency in 1999.

● Spotlight

In 1992, the Committee on the Environment, Public Health and Consumer Protection introduced an EU eco-label for environmentally friendly products. The Euro-flower was awarded to companies making 'green' goods including washing machines, soap powders and light bulbs.

The Court of Justice

The European Court of Justice is based in Luxembourg and has fifteen judges, one from each member state, helped by 9 senior lawyers. The Court sees that member states follow the policies set out in the Treaties. It can issue penalties and fines to member states who fail to follow EU laws. Any European citizen can bring a case to the Court, and it has powers to overturn decisions made in or by that citizen's own country.

◀ *Neil Kinnock is the European Commissioner for Administrative Reforms.*

 # Problem

The EU is such a large organization that many Europeans feel they do not know enough about the way it works. The Commission has been criticised for bad management and dishonesty. On 15th March 1999, the European Parliament forced the entire Commission to resign. The Vice President of the Commission, Neil Kinnock, is now in charge of finding ways to reform it.

The EU budget

The EU receives money from its member states, who pay according to how rich they are. Income also comes from duties on goods imported from outside the EU and from a small part of VAT. The Commission works out a draft budget which the Council and Parliament consider. The European Parliament has the power to adopt or reject the budget.

The Commission, the Council and Parliament all consult with special committees and working parties before allocating budgets. There are around 300 special committees covering areas such as agriculture, industry, the environment and food safety.

▼ *Dublin's docklands in the Temple Bar area have been redeveloped as a commercial centre with the help of money from the EU budget.*

4. Agriculture

When the European Community was formed, one of its main aims was to make sure that there would be no more food shortages in Europe as there had been after the Second World War. Agricultural policies aimed to make farming more efficient, and to achieve fair prices for consumers and farmers. The Common Agricultural Policy (CAP) was introduced in 1962. It set out to control amounts of food produced, give grants to farmers and buy up goods to keep prices steady.

▼ Large, prairie-like fields of grain crops have become a familiar part of the European landscape as a result of the Common Agricultural Policy.

▲ *CAP policies have led to surplus crops, like these plum tomatoes grown in Italy.*

▼ *EU quotas limit the amount of milk that a dairy farm can produce each year.*

Changing farming methods

CAP subsidies meant that farmers received a fixed price for their produce. If the butter, grain or wine they produced was not sold, it was bought and stored by the EU or sold or given away. This guarantee of income meant that farmers could produce single crops rather than having to practise mixed farming. CAP grants also encouraged farmers to use intensive methods of farming. They took out hedgerows to make fields larger, drained marshland, and used more fertilisers, pesticides and irrigation.

Intensive farming means that more food is available all year at cheaper prices, but it also has environmental costs. Rivers and soil have been polluted with chemicals, soil has been washed away and wildlife habitats and wetland sites lost. The policy of buying and storing produce to keep prices up led to huge surpluses: grain and butter mountains and oil, milk and wine lakes.

▲ *Surplus food supplies like this 'apple mountain' accumulate when countries over-produce certain foods. The EU is trying to prevent such wastage from occurring.*

During the 1980s, the European Community introduced milk quotas (an amount of food production that is regulated according to need) and other 'stabilisers' to limit the amount that farmers produced. To encourage less intensive production, farmers were paid compensation for taking some of their land out of production as 'set aside' for five years or more.

In 1992, there were reforms to the Common Agricultural Policy. Prices for cereals, oil seeds and beef were reduced to keep European produce competitive on the world market. More farmers were given grants for set aside, and for planting trees.

▶ *European farmers are being encouraged to use fields to grow young trees for timber to reduce over-production of crops.*

Problem

CAP reforms mean that subsidies (financial help) to European farmers have been reduced. Farmers have protested against cuts in subsidies and land being taken out of production. But some people believe that subsidies led to surpluses, waste and high food prices that made it hard for developing countries to compete on the world market.

In 1999, further reforms were made to the Common Agricultural Policy. They set out these main aims for the future:

- To modernise farms
- To improve the safety and quality of food products
- To ensure a fair and stable income for farmers
- To protect the environment
- To create new jobs in rural areas
- To improve living and working conditions

Changing fishing methods

European fisheries have come under increasing pressure with the growing demand for fish, and some North Sea herring and cod fisheries have been nearly used up. The EU is laying down new guidelines for the fishing industry for the years to 2006, to establish a balance between the growing demand for fish and the need to conserve stocks in the seas.

▲ *To conserve dwindling fish stocks, under-sized fish are thrown back into the sea.*

▼ *A Spanish trawler is escorted back to Plymouth after being arrested on suspicion of illegal fishing in English waters.*

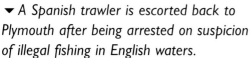

Problem

The Common Fisheries Policy set quotas for fishing vessels and limited fishing in coastal zones to try and save falling fish stocks. It has been criticised because it means dead fish are thrown back into the sea when quotas are used up. Some people feel that fish stocks will only be saved by reducing the number of EU fishing vessels and introducing a licensing scheme for fishing vessels.

5. Trade and industry

In the **EU** today, most wealth comes from service industries like telecommunications, banking and tourism. There has also been an increase in light industries such as the manufacture of plastics and hi-tech machinery. Most jobs in the **EU** are in the service and manufacturing industries. Agriculture now accounts for less than 8 per cent of total employment.

EU policies aim to encourage trade and industry and reduce poverty. Grants are given to improve transport and the environment in poorer areas to encourage new industry there. The EU aims to reduce unemployment in all its countries to around 5 per cent. In 1989, EU member states signed the Social Charter, giving European citizens certain social rights in employment, training and the working environment.

▲ EU transport policies have encouraged the building of new roads to improve trade and communication. For example, it has invested in the construction of the Oresund road bridge linking Denmark and Sweden.

▲ The Eurostar train offers a high-speed link between the UK and European cities for business and leisure passengers.

 Spotlight

The EU introduced the Single Market in 1993 to encourage trade within the EU. The Single Market means that goods can be transported from one country to another within the EU without paying duties. For example, a car made in Germany should cost the same whether it is sold in Belgium or Italy. EU transport policies aim to encourage trade in the Single Market by establishing high-speed road and rail links across the EU. A network of motorways and high-speed rail links is planned for completion by 2010.

Problem

EU imports include raw materials like iron ore from Brazil, and food products like bananas from the Caribbean. Multi-national companies often own the companies that process, ship and sell the goods. This means that they can control the prices, forcing poorer countries to sell at low prices to stay in business. Some people argue that the EU helps developing countries to earn currency through trade, but others feel it would be better to help poorer countries develop their own trade and industry.

▲ Bananas imported from the Caribbean are unloaded at a European port.

◄ Timber from the Amazon region of South America is loaded onto a ship to be transported to Europe.

Problem

The EU's Common Agricultural Policy, which gives directives on farming practices and prices, is not always popular with European farmers. For example, in 1999 more than 2000 French farmers in tractors staged a demonstration outside the European Parliament building in Strasbourg in protest against the Agricultural Policy. In the same year, another group of angry French farmers protested against the EU's low price settings by blocking busy trading routes, such as the entrance to the Eurotunnel.

▲ *French farmers block a main road near the Eurotunnel entrance in protest against the European Agricultural Policy.*

▲ *An abattoir worker sprays a permanent yellow dye on the carcasses of British cattle infected by BSE to ensure that they are destroyed and cannot be sold or eaten.*

Problem

After the outbreak of "Mad Cow Disease" or BSE in the UK in the late 1980s, the EU Commission banned the export of all UK British cattle and meat products. The British government took stringent measures to combat BSE and convince the European Commission that British beef was safe. The European Commission carried out regular inspections in the UK before lifting the ban in the summer of 1999. But France went against the EU ruling and refused to accept British beef because it was still worried about its safety. As a result, the EU is taking legal action against the government of France.

6. European law

The Treaties made between European Union countries on different subjects are the Constitution of the European Union and the basis for all its laws.

▲ *The European Court of Justice occupies a large modern building in Luxembourg.*

Treaties set out aims for EU policies and also timetables. The Treaties must be accepted by every state that applies to join the EU. They have been revised at meetings held at Maastricht and Amsterdam and are amended when new member states

join the EU. The laws based on EU Treaties can over-rule the laws of individual countries.

The European Commission makes proposals for new laws, after consulting with special committees and 'working parties', which are made

discussion on subjects like Social Policy or the Single Currency. These can lead to White Papers which are practical proposals for laws. Some EU laws, like regulations and decisions, must be enforced by all member states. Others, like directives, set out aims which member states can achieve in their own way.

The Commission must see that EU laws are followed. It has powers to take member governments to the European Court of Justice if they fail to follow EU laws.

Lobbyists

Lobbyists and Pressure Groups are people who work for a special cause, like animal welfare, the environment, or human rights. They argue their case to politicians and try to influence the making of policies and laws. Many of these groups have a base in Brussels so they can argue their case to Members of the European Parliament (MEPs) or members of the committees who advise the EU on policy.

up of government and other experts. Proposals are then debated in the European Parliament, before the Council of Ministers takes decisions on new laws in consultation with Parliament.

The Commission produces Green Papers which are documents for

The European Court of Justice

The European Court of Justice is based in Luxembourg. Its main role is to see that laws based on the Treaties are followed throughout the EU. If a government or company fails to follow EU laws, the Court can impose fines or penalties. Any citizen of the EU can bring a case to the Court. It can over-rule national laws and there is no appeal against its decisions.

Spotlight

The Bosman ruling

In September 1995, Belgian football player Jean-Marc Bosman took his case to the European Court of Justice. He claimed his football career was ruined by the failure of his team FC Liege to honour a transfer agreement for him to move to French club Dunkerque. The court ruled in his favour and the case changed football history. The 'Bosman ruling' means that football clubs can no longer charge an excessive transfer fee for players wishing to switch clubs.

 ## Spotlight

The Francovich case

Mr Francovich was an employee of an Italian firm that went bankrupt. A 1980 EC directive gave protection to employees following a firm's bankruptcy but the Italian government had failed to put it into effect. The Court of Justice ruled that Mr Francovich could claim compensation from the Italian government.

▼ Belgian football player Jean-Marc Bosman (centre) and his lawyers hold a press conference following his hearing at the European Court of Justice.

7. Money

Europe has one of the strongest economies in the world. EU economic policies aim to make the EU more effective when it trades with other parts of the world and to protect member states from the risk of sudden changes in the value of their currency.

The European Monetary System (EMS) was set up in 1979 to make exchange rates and interest rates more stable in Europe and to bring the monetary policies of member states closer together. This is to prepare them for European Monetary Union (EMU) and a Single Currency.

Exchange Rate Mechanism (ERM)

The ERM is part of the European Monetary System. Its aim is to keep exchange rates between European currencies steady. This helps European businesses because they are not at risk from their own country's currencies suddenly getting stronger or weaker. Those countries that have joined the ERM have their currencies fixed against each other and against the European Currency Unit, the euro. If they go up or down beyond the limits that have been fixed, currencies are bought or sold or interest rates raised or lowered to bring them back into line with the ERM.

 ## Problem

The UK pound sterling joined the ERM in October 1990, but on Wednesday 16th September 1992, frantic speculation over currencies caused by high German interest rates led to a serious fall in the value of the pound. In order to raise it back to acceptable levels the Treasury would have to spend large sums of money. Rather than do this, the UK left the ERM on a day that became known as Black Wednesday.

▶ *On Black Wednesday the Chancellor, Norman Lamont, announced that Britain was leaving the ERM.*

All the member states of the EU – 13 in total – have joined the ERM except for Sweden and the UK. All countries that want to join have to show that their economies are strong enough.

The Treaty of Maastricht

The Treaty of Maastricht was signed at a meeting of the European Council in December 1991. The Treaty set out three stages towards European Monetary Union (EMU) but allowed opt-outs for Denmark and the UK.

◀ A banknote for the euro, Europe's single currency.

The Single Currency

The euro is the official currency of the EU. Twelve countries have adopted it by joining the ERM. This means their own currencies count as units of the euro, and have a fixed exchange rate against it. From 1999, the euro began to be used as a trading currency by businesses and the international money markets, and the issue of euro banknotes and coins is set for 1st January 2002. Countries within the euro zone can trade with each other without changing currencies, which means that business costs are lower and companies are not at risk from changes in the value of their country's currency.

▼ In January 1999, the euro was launched at the European Central Bank in Frankfurt. As part of festivities to mark the occasion, thousands of people gathered around a large euro sign.

● Spotlight

Many business people throughout Europe want to join the Single Currency because they believe it will help their businesses. There are also a large number of consumers throughout Europe who are in favour of the Single Currency because it means they could compare prices more easily when abroad. Other people want to keep their own currency and are worried that joining the Single Currency will mean that they have to give away their economic powers to a European Superstate. They fear that this will mean they have less say in what happens to their country's economy in the future.

▶ *Big Ben and the Houses of Parliament are to many a symbol of the UK's sovereignty.*

In the future, the EU could change in a number of ways. Some of the issues it faces were outlined in Agenda 2000, an action programme adopted by the Commission on 15th July 1997.
They include:

Enlargement

As more countries in central and eastern Europe apply to join, the EU could grow. This growth is called enlargement. Negotiations began in 1998 for six countries who wish to join – Cyprus, the Czech Republic, Estonia, Hungary, Poland and Slovenia – about the terms of their membership. Since then, a further seven countries have applied for membership: Bulgaria, Latvia, Lithuania, Malta, Romania, Slovakia and Turkey. Countries that want to join the EU must show that they have:

- Democratic government and political stability
- A free market economy (in which competition in the market place is not restricted)
- Commitment to the EU's political, economic and monetary aims
- Acceptance of EU laws

Some people want the EU to grow to include more European countries. Others believe that before it can grow bigger, it needs to make its institutions and powers stronger. Many feel that if the EU enlarges to include twenty or more countries, its institutions will need to undergo reform to represent the increased number of countries adequately.

 Spotlight

In 2000, the EU broke off relations with Austria because the government there included the ultra right-wing Freedom Party. Europeans were concerned about the Party's fascist ideas, which reminded people of Adolf Hitler and Nazi Germany. Hitler's government persecuted minority groups, such as Jews, taking away their rights and systematically destroying them. EU relations were resumed once Austria made it clear that its government still respected the rights of minorities and immigrants.

▼ *Jörg Haider, leader of the far-right Freedom Party in Austria.*

Political union

The EU could become a political union which means that member states would share one central European government. Some see EMU as a step towards this. Political union means transferring more powers from national governments to EU institutions.

This raises the question of sovereignty. Sovereignty means that a country's government can act independently. Some people believe that national governments should keep power, especially in areas like defence and foreign affairs, and the issue of currency. Because of these concerns, The Treaty of Maastricht states that decisions must be taken at national, regional or local level within a country except where they need to be taken at European Community level to be effective.

▼ The civil war between Serbs and Croats made Bosnia one of the most troubled areas of Europe and a major cause for concern to the EU.

Peace in Europe

Since the Second World War, the threat to peace in Europe has come from disputes between groups of people from different races or religions like those in Bosnia Herzegovina and Kosovo in the former Yugoslavia, and from groups who want to break away from national governments and rule themselves.

The EU is trying to reduce trouble in Central and Eastern Europe by investing in efforts to modernise agriculture and industry.

- The EU has spent about 1.2 billion euros helping the economies of central and eastern Europe.
- The EU is the world's largest donor of food aid to developing countries.
- The EU has spent 397 million euros on education, training and youth projects.

In global terms, the EU has become a strong economic unit but it does not represent a political force yet. Member states are working together to develop the Western European Union (WEU) as the defence arm of the EU. WEU members agree to make military forces available to defend European countries to help in peacekeeping or rescue tasks.

▼ The EU sends food and hygiene parcels to areas like Bosnia that are suffering as a result of war or natural disasters.

Wildlife preservation

The EU does not merely concern itself with the interests of its citizens. As problems facing the environment become ever more pressing, the EU is also involved in wildlife protection initiatives. For example, the Royal Society for the Protection of Birds (RSPB) in the UK works with similar organizations within the European Union to monitor the numbers and safe passage of birds crossing the continent during migration.

▶ *A young bittern is ringed for an RSPB project funded by the EU to monitor the birds' migration.*

Future citizens

The EU runs educational and training programmes to improve opportunities for young people and to encourage travel and exchanges between European member states. The Tempus Programme organizes exchanges between young people from the EU and the countries of central and eastern Europe, and Socrates funds courses in schools, universities and language centres. Youth For Europe III helps young people join local training projects. Today's children and young people are the future citizens of Europe. They will help shape the EU in a fast-changing world.

▶ *A Swedish student addresses students from other member states during a Euroschool day at the European Parliament in Strasbourg.*

Glossary

budget — the amount of income and spending for a year

citizen — a member of a city, town or country or larger community

constitution — a document written down when an organization is formed

currency — coins and notes used as money

duties — an amount of money paid as tax to a government

enlargement — the word used to describe the EU growing to include more member states

euro — the official currency of the EU

European Commission — a body of representatives from member states which plans and manages policy and proposes new legislation

European Council — the supreme decision-making body of the EU

European Parliament — the elected assembly of MEPs

fisheries — areas of coastal waters and seas where fish are caught

free market economy — an economy in which prices are fixed by competition

green paper — a document containing information to encourage debate on an issue.

lobbyists — people who campaign for a cause, such as animal welfare or the environment

Ombudsman — a watchdog – someone who looks into complaints

quota — the amount or share allowed

referendum — when the people of a country vote to make a decision

Single Market — the trade between member states which excludes payment of duties

subsidy — a grant of money made to boost trade or development

treaty — a formal agreement made and signed by state governments

veto — the right to block a decision

WEU — The Western European Union – an organization set up to encourage cooperation between European countries on defence and security matters.

white paper — a document containing practical proposals for action on an issue

Useful addresses and websites

European Parliament UK Office
2 Queen Anne's Gate
London
SWIH 9AA

Office for the Official Publications of the European Communities
European Commission
2 rue Mercier
2985 Luxembourg

European Information Centres (EICs) can be found in most member states oof the European Union. In the UK, they can be found in many cities. Try contacting the London branch for a list of centres.
Euro Info Centre
London Chamber of Commerce and Industry
33 Queen Street
London EC4R JAP

www.europa.eu.int
comprehensive website for EU, with links to other sites

www.euroguide.org
an A to Z guide on the EU on the Internet

www.eurunion.org/profile/home.htm
a guide to the EU giving facts and figures compared with the US

www.europa.eu.int/euro
a guide to the Euro currency

www.cec.org.uk
website for the European Commission Representation in London

www.ecu-notes.org
an a to z of EU terms

www. eia.org.uk
website for the European Information Assocation

www.europa.eu.int/scadplus
glossary of key issues and policies

Index